This workbook covers the microeconomics topics which are not in the AS specification.

As all exam boards are slightly different you may have covered some of these topics or covered them in less detail at AS level.

The specification links refer to the A level specification.
- AQA Individuals, firms, markets and market failure (7136)
- CIE Paper 3 (9708)
- Edexcel Theme 3 Business behavior and the labour market (9ECO)
- OCR Microeconomics (H460/01)

	AQA	CIE	Edexcel	OCR
Chapter 1	4.1.4.2	2e 2f	3.1.1 3.1.2 3.1.3 3.2.1	3.1
Chapter 2	4.1.4.3 4.1.4.4 4.1.4.5 4.1.4.6 4.1.4.7 4.1.4.8	2c	3.3.1 3.3.2 3.3.3 3.3.4	3.2 3.3
Chapter 3	4.1.5.1 4.1.5.10	1a 2a 2b 2d	3.4.1 3.4.7	4.1 4.2 4.4 4.4 4.5
Chapter 4	4.1.4.3	2d	3.4.2	4.1
Chapter 5	4.1.5.4 4.1.5.8	2d	3.4.3	4.3
Chapter 6	4.1.4.4	2d	3.4.4	4.4
Chapter 7	4.1.4.6 4.1.5.7 4.1.5.8	2d	3.4.5 3.4.6	4.2
Chapter 8	4.1.5.9		3.4.7	4.5
Chapter 9	4.1.6.1 4.1.6.2	3c	3.5.1 3.5.2 3.5.3	5.1 5.2
Chapter 10	4.1.6.3 4.1.6.4 4.1.6.5	3c	3.5.3	5.3
Chapter 11	4.1.6.6 4.1.6.7		3.5.3 3.6.1 3.6.2	
Chapter 12		1b 1c		
Chapter 13		3a 3d		
Chapter 14	4.1.7.1 4.1.7.2 4.1.7.3	3b		
Chapter 15	4.1.2.3 4.1.2.4			

Contents

Chapter 1	Business Objectives and Growth	4
Chapter 2	Costs, Revenue and Profit	9
Chapter 3	Market Structures Introduction	18
Chapter 4	Perfect Competition	23
Chapter 5	Monopolistic Competition	27
Chapter 6	Oligopoly	31
Chapter 7	Monopoly	35
Chapter 8	Contestable Markets	43
Chapter 9	Demand and Supply of Labour	46
Chapter 10	Wage Determination and Trade Unions	53
Chapter 11	Discrimination and Government Intervention	60
Chapter 12	Externalities and Market Failure	66
Chapter 13	Policies to Achieve Efficient Resource Allocation	74
Chapter 14	Income and Wealth Redistribution	83
Chapter 15	Behavioral Economics	87

Chapter 1 Business Objectives and Growth

1. What is usually the main objective of a firm? (1)

2. What is the 'rule' for revenue maximisation? (1)

3. Why might a firm choose this objective? (1)

4. What is the 'rule' for sales maximisation? (1)

5. Why might a firm choose this objective? (1)

6. Draw a diagram to show the above 3 objectives (3)

7. Under what circumstances might a firm be happy accepting a loss? (2)

8. Explain the concept of satisficing using an example (2)

9. Give two more additional objectives firms might have (2)

10. For each firm state and explain what is likely to be their objective in the short run (10)

a) a school

b) A newly opened restaurant

c) A well established restaurant

d) Oxfam

e) A family run shop

11. Explain making use of an example, the meaning of 'divorce or ownership from control' (3)

Edexcel only

12. Give two reasons why firms grow (2)

13. Give two reasons why some firms want to stay small (2)

15. Explain with an example the meaning of horizontal integration (2)

16. Explain with an example the meaning of vertical integration (2)

17. Give an example of forward vertical integration (1)

18. Give a reason for forward vertical integration (1)

19. Give an example of backward vertical integration (1)

20. Give a reason for backward vertical integration (1)

21. Explain the meaning of conglomerate giving an example (2)

22. Explain the meaning of organic growth (1)

23. **Explain** three disadvantages of growth to the firm (6)

24. Give two advantages of growth to consumers (2)

25. Give two disadvantages of growth to consumers (2)

26. Explain the meaning of demerger (2)

27. **Explain** four reasons for demergers (8)

28. Give two benefits of demergers for workers (2)

29. Give two benefits of demergers for consumers (2)

30. For each example state the type of integration (4)
a) two supermarkets joining together

b) a restaurant takes over a farm

c) a clothing retailer merges with a fast food restaurant
d)

e) A car manufacturer taking over a car retailer

Chapter 2 Costs, Revenue and Profit

1. Define fixed costs (2)

   Expenses that do not change dependant on output

2. Define variable costs (2)

   Expenses that do change dependant on output

3. For each business give **two** examples of fixed costs and **two** examples of variable costs (10)

a) A doctors surgery

   F - Rent, wage of staff
   V - Medical supplies, utility bills

b) A hotel

   F - Property insurance, maintanence of building
   V - Laundry service, food and drink for guests

c) A school

   F - Wages of teachers, building maintanence
   V - Educational materials, utility bills

d) A gym

   F - Rent, wage for staff
   V - Cleaning supplies, energy cost

e) A bank

   F - Wages of staff, Rent
   V - Office supplies, utility bills

4. Define and give the formula for average cost (3)

The cost per unit of output
$AC = \frac{TC}{Q}$

5. Define marginal cost (2)

The additional cost incurred when producing one more unit of output

6. Draw a diagram showing AC and MC (3)

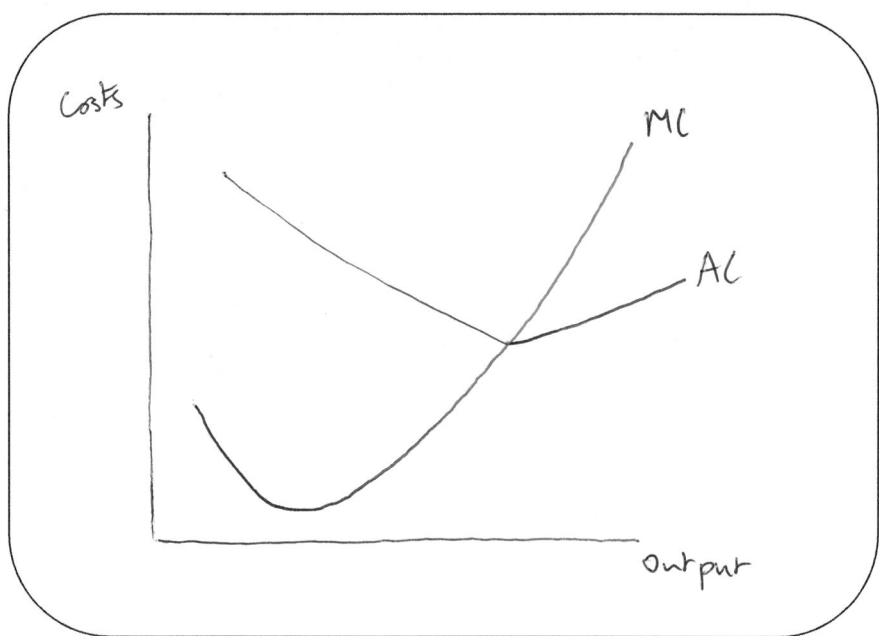

7. What is the key relationship between these two curves? (1)

When MC is below AC, AC is decreasing and when MC is above AC, AC is increasing

8. What is the difference between short run and long run? (2)

- In the short run at least one factor of production is fixed
- In the long run all factors of production are variable

9. Explain the meaning of total product? (1)

10. Explain the meaning of marginal product (1)

11. Give the formula for average product (1)

12. State the law of diminishing returns (2)

If you add more variable inputs to a fixed input, the additional output produced will eventually decrease due to inefficiency

14. Explain using an example, why marginal product will eventually decline (3)

15. Draw a diagram to show the relationship between MC and MP (3)

16. Explain why MC increases as MP falls (2)

Q17-19 AQA only

17. Draw a diagram to show the relationship between MP and AP (3)

18. At what point on the above diagram does productivity fall? (1)

19. Explain two ways in which productivity could be improved (2)

20. Define economies of scale (2)

21. What is the difference between internal and external economies of scale? (2)

22. For each business **explain** two different economics of scale they could benefit from (20)

a) A school

b) A gym

c) A pub

d) McDonalds

e) A clothing store

23. Define diseconomies of scale (2)

24. Explain two diseconomies of scale (4)

25. Draw an AC curve, on this curve show economies and diseconomies of scale (2)

26. Explain why there are large economics of scale when the fixed costs are high (2)

27. Draw a diagram to show the relationship between the short run and long run average cost curve (4)

28. Explain why there are multiple short run average cost curves on your diagram (2)

29. Explain the impact of external economies of scale on the LRAC curve (1)

30. Draw a diagram to show minimum efficient scale of production and optimal range of output (2)

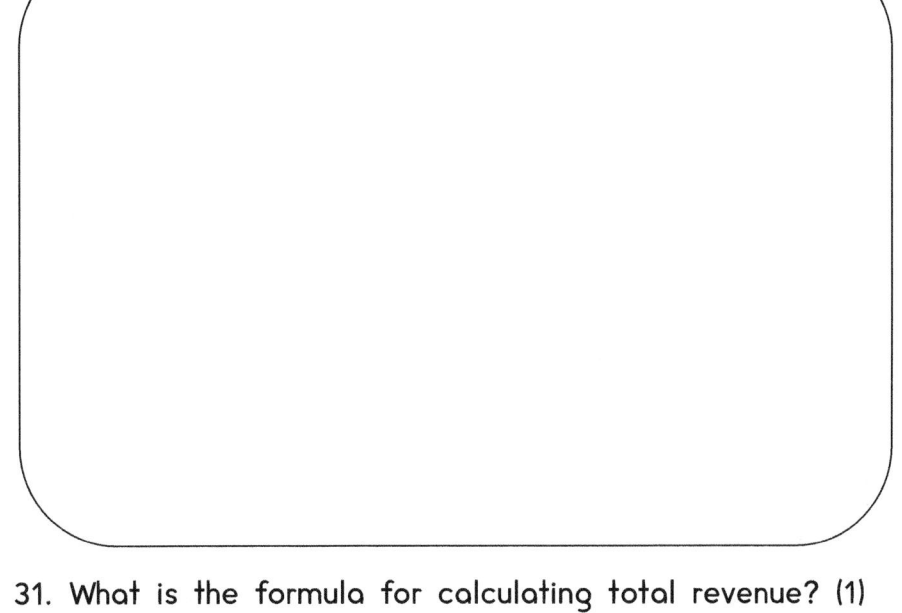

31. What is the formula for calculating total revenue? (1)

TR = P × Q

32. What is the formula for calculating average revenue? (1)

AR = TR/Q

33. Define normal profit (2)

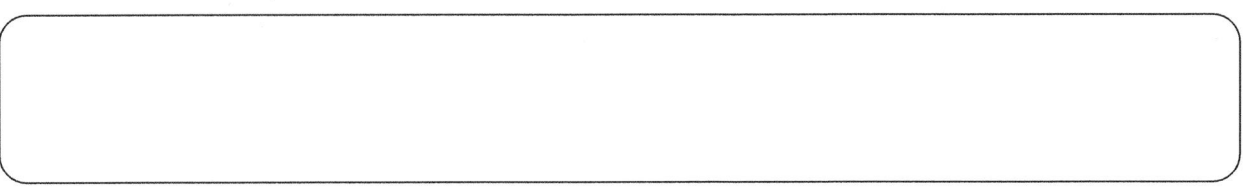

34. Define supernormal profit (1)

35. What is the relationship between TC and TR when normal profit is made? (1)

36. What is the rule for profit maximisation? (1)

A firm can maximise output where MC = MR

37. Draw a diagram to show the relationship between AR, MR and TR (5)

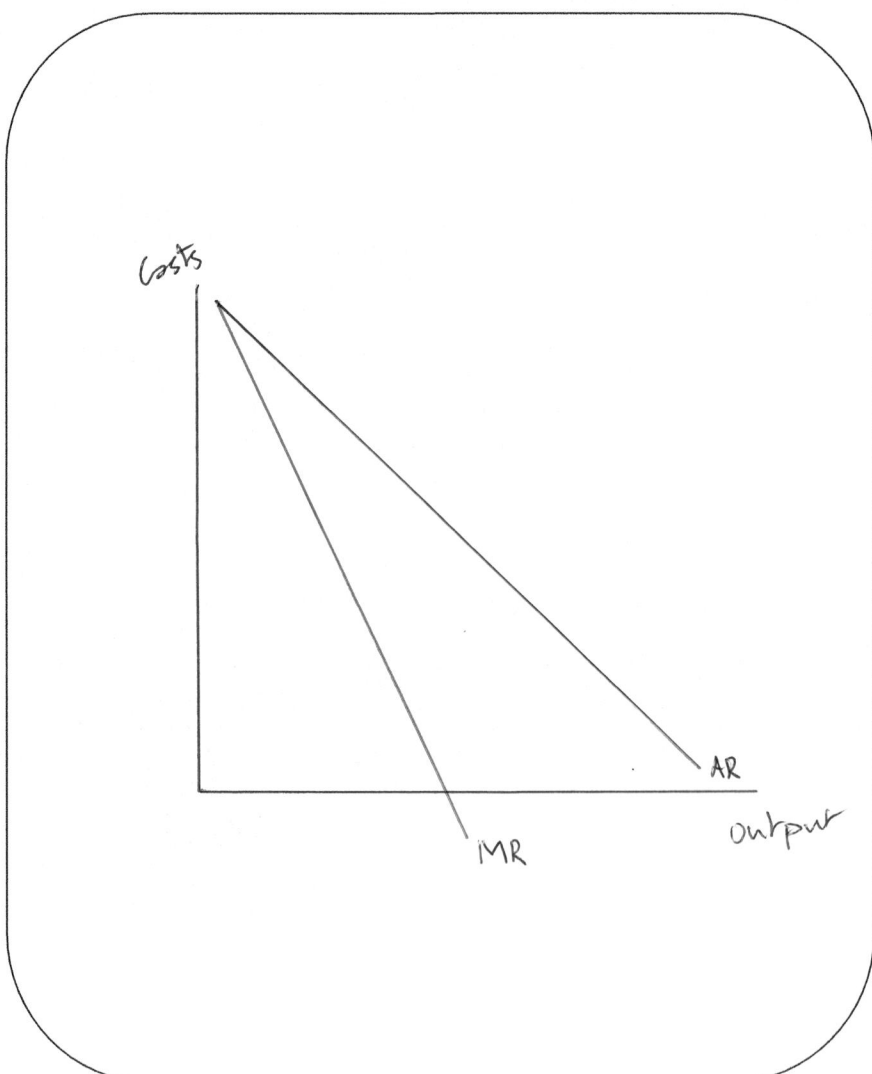

38. Draw a demand curve, on your diagram label inelastic demand, elastic demand and unitary elastic demand (3)

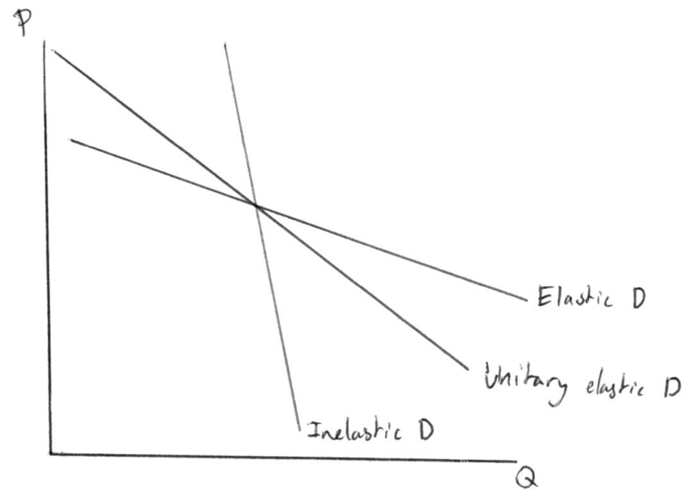

39 If a firm is making a loss they may continue to produce in the short run, under what circumstances would they produce in the short run? Explain your answer (3)

<u>AQA only</u>

40. What is the difference between innovation and invention? (2)

41. Explain how improved technology impacts costs of production (3)

42. Explain how technological change can lead to creative destruction giving an example (3)

Chapter 3 Market Structures Introduction

1. Explain the meaning of the phrase 'barriers to entry' (1)

2. What is the meaning of 'incumbent' firm? (1)

3. How do barriers to entry help incumbent firms? (1)

4. Explain why brand loyalty acts as a barrier to entry (1)

5. Explain giving an example why high sunk costs act as a barrier to entry (2)

6. Explain the pricing strategies that incumbent firms could follow to prevent new firms entering (4)

7. Give two examples of barriers to entry which are due to government regulations?

8. For each industry state two likely barriers to entry (20)
a) supermarket

b) Bank

c) Private school

d) Fast food restaurant

e) Pub

f) Corner shop

g) Window cleaner

h) A personal trainer

i) An economics tutor

j) Soft drinks industry

9. Define homogenous product and give an example (2)

10. Define differentiated product and give an example (2)

11. What does it mean by perfect information? (2)

12. Define allocative efficiency (2)

13. Define productive efficiency (2)

14. Define dynamic efficiency (2)

15. Define static efficiency (2)

Q16- 20 CIE A level; other exam boards AS (year 12)

16. What does it mean by making rational decisions? (2)

17. Give two examples of situations when a consumer might not make a rational decision (2)

18. Explain with an example the meaning of utility (2)

19. What does marginal utility mean? (1)

20. Using the concept of marginal utility explain why a consumer eats more at an all you can eat pizza buffet than if they were paying per slice (3)

Q21-24 CIE only

20. What does a budget line show? (2)

21. What does an indifference curve show? (2)

22. Draw a diagram of an indifference curve and budget line showing where the consumer will consume (3)

23. On your diagram show what will happen if the price of the good on the X axes increases (2)

24. On your diagram show the income and substitution effect (2)

Chapter 4 Perfect Competition

1. How many firms are there in a perfectly competitive industry? (1)

2. What type of product is produced in a perfectly competitive industry? (1)

3. What can you say about the barriers to entry in a perfectly competitive industry? (1)

4. Is there perfect knowledge in a perfectly competitive industry? (1)

5. Are firms price makers or price takers? (1)

6. Draw a diagram to show a perfectly competitive firm making supernormal profit (3)

7. Explain why this is only a short run situation (2)

8. Draw a diagram of the **firm and industry** to show what will happen in the long run if supernormal profit is made (5)

9. Draw a diagram to show a perfectly competitive firm making a loss (3)

10. Draw a diagram of the firm and industry to show what will happen in the long run if losses are made (5)

11. Explain using a diagram why perfect competition is productively efficient in the long run (3)

12. Explain why firms in perfect competition are X-efficient (2)

13. Explain whether perfect competition leads to allocative efficiency (2)

14. **Explain** two reasons why perfect competition does not lead to dynamic efficiency (4)

15. Explain why static efficiency is achieved (2)

16. **Explain** three policies the government could use to try to increase competition in markets (6)

Chapter 5 Monopolistic Competition

1. How many firms are there in monopolistic competition? (1)

2. Give an example of a monopolistically competitive industry (1)

3. What type of product is produced in a monopolistic competition? (1)

4. What can you say about the barriers to entry in monopolistic competition? (1)

5. Are firms price makers or price takers? Explain why (2)

6. Draw a diagram to show a monopolistically competitive firm making supernormal profit (3)

7. Explain why this is only a short run situation (2)

8. Draw a diagram to show what will happen in the long run if supernormal profit is made (5)

9. Draw a diagram to show a monopolistically competitive firm making a loss (3)

10. Draw a diagram to show what will happen in the long run if losses are made (5)

11. Explain using a diagram why monopolistic competition is not productively efficient (3)

12. **Explain** whether firms are X-efficient (2)

13. **Explain** whether monopolistic competition leads to allocative efficiency (2)

14. Explain two reasons why monopolistic competition does not lead to dynamic efficiency (4)

15. **Explain** under what circumstances monopolistic competition might be dynamically efficient (2)

16. **Explain** whether static efficiency is achieved (2)

17. How would you expect prices in monopolistic competition to compare to perfect competition? Explain your answer (3)

Chapter 6 Oligopoly

1. How many firms are there in oligopoly? (1)

2. Give an example of an oligopolistic industry (1)

3. Explain what it means by a 3 firm concentration ratio (2)

4. What type of product is produced in oligopoly? (1)

5. What can you say about the barriers to entry in oligopoly? (1)

6. Is there perfect knowledge in oligopoly? (1)

7. What type of profits are made in the short run? (1)

8. What type of profits are made in the long run? Explain your answer (2)

9. Explain what is meant by non-price competition giving two examples (3)

10. Why do oligopolistic firms use non-price competition? (2)

11. Is there productive efficiency in oligopoly? (1)

12. Explain whether oligopoly leads to allocative efficiency (2)

13. Explain what the term collusion means and why it is found in oligopoly (3)

14. Explain the difference between formal and informal (tacit) collusion (2)

15. **Explain** two factors oligopolies might collude on. (4)

16. **Explain** two benefits to producers of colluding (4)

17. Explain two problems to consumers of firms colluding (4)

18. Draw a diagram of the demand curve (AR) and MR curve for oligopoly (3)

19. Explain why the demand curve has two sections (4)

Edexcel only

20. **Explain** using a game theory matrix what the game theory model shows (6)

21. Explain using your matrix why one firm might be tempted to 'cheat'? (3)

22. How can 'cheating' be avoided in the game theory model? (1)

Chapter 7 Monopoly

1. How many firms are there in a pure monopoly? (1)

2. What type of product is produced in a monopoly? (1)

3. What can you say about the barriers to entry in monopoly? (1)

4. Is there perfect knowledge in monopoly? (1)

5. Are firms price makers or price takers? (1)

6. Draw a diagram to show a monopoly making supernormal profit (3)

7. Explain why this is a long run situation (2)

8. Draw a diagram to show monopoly making a loss (3)

9. If monopoly is making a loss, why might they not be able to leave immediately? (1)

10. Sometimes a monopoly may choose to continue to produce in the short run even though they are making a loss. Under what circumstances would they be better off producing than not producing despite a loss being made? (2)

11. Draw a diagram to show a monopoly which will continue to produce in the short run despite a loss being made (you will need to include an AVC) (3)

12. Draw a diagram to show a monopoly which will shut down immediately when a loss is made (you will need to include an AVC) (3)

13. Explain whether monopoly is productively efficient (2)

14. Explain why firms in monopoly is likely to be X-inefficient (2)

15. Explain whether monopoly leads to allocative efficiency (2)

16. Explain two reasons why monopoly does not lead to dynamic efficiency (4)

17. Explain two reasons why monopoly might lead to dynamic efficiency (4)

18. Explain why static efficiency is not achieved (2)

19. Give two benefits to firms of monopoly (2)

20. Give two benefits to consumers of monopoly (2)

21. Give two benefits to employees of monopoly (2)

22. Give two benefits to suppliers of monopoly (2)

23. Give two costs to firms of monopoly (2)

24. Give two costs to consumers of monopoly (2)

25. Give two costs to employees of monopoly (2)

26. Give two costs to suppliers of monopoly (2)

27. Define natural monopoly giving an example (3)

28. Draw a diagram to illustrate natural monopoly (2)

29. Explain why a government would be reluctant to break up a natural monopoly (2)

30. Explain the meaning of monopsony giving an example (2)

31. Which economic agent benefits most from a monopsony? Explain your answer (2)

32. Which economic agent suffers most from a monopsony? Explain your answer (2)

33. Define (3rd degree) price discrimination (2)

34. Give two examples of price discrimination (2)

35. Draw diagrams to show how firms' total revenue will increase if they use price discrimination (4)

36. Draw diagrams to show the impact on consumer surplus when price discrimination is used (4)

37. Give two benefits to consumers of price discrimination (2)

38. Give two disadvantages to consumers of price discrimination (2)

39. What are two conditions necessary in order for firms to be able to make use of price discrimination (2)

40. What is first degree price discrimination (2)

41. Why is first degree price discrimination unlikely to happen in real life? (2)

42. What is second degree price discrimination? (2)

Explain why firms use second degree price discrimination (2

Chapter 8 Contestable Markets

1. What does it mean by a contestable market? (1)

2. Which market structure by definition will always be contestable and why? (2)

3. Can supernormal profits be made in the short run? (1)

4. Can supernormal profits be made in the long run? (1)

5. Explain why incumbent firms sometimes set prices lower than profit max price? (2)

6. For each question **explain** whether the firm becomes more or less contestable (6)
a) patents are cheaper and easier to get

b) Incumbent firms have high brand loyalty

c) Second hand machinery is more expensive

d) Incumbent firms spend more on advertising

e) There is threat of limit pricing by incumbent firms

f) Capital equipment falls in price

7. Explain the meaning of hit and run tactics (2)

8. Explain the meaning of limit pricing and why it is used (3)

9. Draw a diagram to show now limit pricing works (3)

10. Explain the meaning of creative destruction (2)

11. Explain why creative destruction is less likely to happen when the market is contestable (2)

Chapter 9 Demand and Supply of Labour

1. Explain with an example why labour is a derived demand (2)

2. What is the meaning of marginal physical product (MPP)? (2)

3. What is the meaning of marginal revenue product (MRP) (2)

4. What is the meaning of marginal cost of labour? (2)

5. Explain why firms will employ workers up to the point where MRP = MC of labour? (2)

6. Explain why MC of labour is perfectly elastic in a perfectly competitive labour market (2)

7. Draw a diagram to show MC of labour and MRP of labour in a perfectly competitive labour market. Show on your diagram the numbers of workers employed (3)

8. Explain, using the concept of diminishing returns, why the MPP curve slopes downwards (2)

9. Explain the meaning of unit labour costs (2)

10. A worker produces 10 units a day and is paid £50 a day. The worker now produces 12 units a day and is still paid the same. What has happened to unit labour costs? (2)

11. Explain two factors which could have brought above this change (4)

12. A worker produces 20 units a day and is paid £80. The worker now produces 25 units. How much should they be paid to maintain the same unit labour cost? (2)

13. What does it mean in terms of unit labour cost if there has been an increase in productivity? (2)

14. In each situation **explain** whether productivity increases or decreases (6)
a) original wage £10 an hour, output 10 units per hour; wage stays the same but output falls to 8 units per hour.

b) Original wage £10 an hour, output 10 units per hour; wage increases to £11 an hour whilst output increases to 12 units per hour.

c) Original wage £10 an hour, output 10 units per hour; wage increases to £12 an hour whilst output increases to 11 units an hour

15. Why is the labour demand curve also the MRP of labour curve? (2)

16. For each situation state and **explain** whether the MRP curve shifts right or left (8)
a) increase in price of the good

b) Increase in the demand for the good

c) New technology to help the worker

d) Increase in training costs of workers

16. Explain the meaning of elastic demand for labour (2)

18. For each situation explain whether the demand for labour is likely to be elastic or inelastic (8)

a) it is easy to use machines instead of workers

b) The demand for the product is elastic

c) Wages are a small proportion of total costs

d) In the long run

18. What is the meaning of labour supply? (1)

19. Draw a diagram showing the supply curve for labour (2)

20. Explain why the supply curve is the shape you have drawn (2)

21. Define and give an example of pecuniary benefits (2)

22. Define and give an example of non-pecuniary benefits (2)

23. Give two reasons why a worker might be prepared to work in job A even though job B might pay more (2)

24. Explain two factors which shift the supply curve for labour to the right (4)

25. Explain why the elasticity of supply of labour is more elastic in low skilled jobs (2)

26. Explain how mobility of labour affects the elasticity of supply of labour (4)

<u>OCR only</u>

27. Draw a diagram showing the backward bending supply curve for labour (2)

28. Explain why the curve is backward bending (2)

Chapter 10 Wage Determination and Trade Unions

1. Give three reasons why doctors are paid more than nurses (3)

2. Give three reasons why a headteacher is paid more than a classroom teacher (3)

3. Draw a diagram to show what will happen to wage rate if there is an increase in immigration (2)

4. Draw a diagram to show what will happen to the wage rate for teachers if there is an increase in the number of school aged children (2)

5. Draw a diagram to show what will happen to the wage rate for personal trainers if there is an increase desire by a population to get fit (2)

6. Draw a diagram to show what will happen to the wage rate for vets of there are more vets (2)

7. What is the difference between real and nominal wage rate (2)

8. Give three characteristics of a perfectly competitive labour market? (3)

9. In a perfectly competitive labour market are firms wage takers or wage makers? (1)

10. Draw two diagrams to show the relationship between equilibrium in the whole labour market and an individual firm (4)

11. What is the meaning of monopsony labour market giving an example (2)

12. Explain why the marginal cost of labour is greater than the wage rate (2)

13. Draw a diagram to show wage determination in a monopsony labour market (4)

14. On your diagram show the wage rate and number of workers employed in a perfectly competitive labour market (2)

Q15-18 OCR and CIE only

15. Define economic rent (2)

16. Define transfer earnings (2)

17. Draw a diagram to show economic rent and transfer earnings (2)

18. On a diagram show what will happen to economic rent and transfer earnings if elasticity of supply becomes more elastic (2)

<u>Not needed for Edexcel</u>

19. Explain the meaning of trade union giving an example (2)

20. What is the meaning of collective bargaining? (1)

21. Explain how trade unions could increase productivity (1)

22. Give two examples of issues in the work place which trade unions may get involved with (2)

23. Draw a diagram to show how a trade union can lead to unemployment (4)

24. Explain why unemployment might not increase if the pay rise is associated with increased productivity (3)

25. Draw a diagram to show how a trade union could increase the wages and employment in a monopsonistic labour market (4)

Chapter 11 Discrimination and Government Intervention

<u>Q1-4 AQA only</u>

1. Define wage discrimination (2)

2. Give 4 examples of wage discrimination (4)

3. Explain why wage discrimination leads to a misallocation of resources (2)

4. Explain using a diagram why wage discrimination leads to increased costs for firms (5)

Q5-8 AQA and Edexcel only

5. Give two aims of the national minimum wage (2)

6. Draw a diagram to show how the NMW leads to unemployment (3)

7. Draw a diagram to show how the level of unemployment will not be so significant if the demand and supply of labour are both inelastic (3)

Edexcel only

8. In addition to unemployment, give two further disadvantages of a NMW (2)

9. Explain the concept of a maximum wage (2)

10. Give two benefits of a maximum wage (2)

11. Give two problems of a maximum wage (2)

12. Draw a diagram to illustrate a maximum wage (3)

13. Give an example of public sector wage setting (1)

14. Explain two problems of restricting pay for public sector doctors (4)

15. Why does the government often intervene in monopoly markets? (2)

16. What is the CMA? (2)

17. Explain how price regulation could be used (2)

18. How does the government regulate profits? (2)

19. Give an example of a quality standard the government could use to regulate schools (1)

20. Give an example of a quality standard the government could use to regulate a restaurant (1)

21. Explain how deregulation makes a market more contestable (2)

22. Explain how privatisation could make the market more competitive (2)

23. How can the government promote small businesses? (2)

24. Explain how nationalisation can protect suppliers and employees (2)

25. Why does the government intervene to control mergers? (2)

26. What would be the impact on each of the following of privatisation? (5)
a) Prices
b) Profit
c) Efficiency
d) Quality
e) Choice

27. What would be the likely impact on each of the following of deregulation? (5)
a) prices
b) Profit
c) Efficiency
d) Quality
e) Choice

28. Explain the meaning of regulatory capture (2)

Chapter 12 – Market Failure and Externalities

CIE Year 2. All other exam boards Year 1 (AS)

1. Define market failure and give an example (2)

2. Define and give an example of a positive externality (2)

3. Define and give an example of a negative externality (2)

4. What is the formula for social cost? (1)

5. What is the formula for social benefit? (1)

6. For each question give (where possible) an example of:
- private cost
- Private benefit
- External cost
- External benefit
-

a) an individual taking recreational drugs (4)

b) an individual eating more fruit and vegetables (4)

c) a private company building a theme park (4)

d) a new restaurant opening in town (4)

e) the local council building a park in town (4)

7. For each question state whether there is underconsumption or overproduction and why (6)

a) Injections

b) Recreational drugs

c) Production of plastic bottles

d) Cough mixture

e) Bananas

f) Education

8 On the same axes draw a MPC and MSC curve (2)

9. Explain why the MPC and MSC curves differ making use of an example (2)

10. On the same exes draw a MPB and MSB curve (2)

11. Explain why the MPB and MSB curves differ making use of an example (2)

12. The free market equilibrium is where ☐ = MPB. The socially optimal is where ☐ = ☐ (3)

13. Why do the two equilibriums in the previous question differ? (1)

14.. Draw a diagram to show why healthcare is under consumed (4)

15.. Draw a diagram to show the overconsumption of cigarettes (4)

16. Draw a digraph to show the overproduction of a chemical factory (4)

17. Draw a diagram to show the underproduction of firms spending on training their workers (4)

18. For each of the four diagrams above shade in the welfare gain or loss (4)

19. What does it mean by asymmetric information? (1)

20. What does it mean by imperfect information? (1)

21. For each question state whether asymmetric information or imperfect information is present (for some questions both will be present). (6)

   a) Health care

   b) Used car sales

   c) Education

d) Antique seller

e) Alcohol

f) Private doctors

22. Explain why imperfect information could lead to overconsumption of a demerit good making use of an example (4)

CIE Only
23. Define cost-benefit analysis (2)

24. What are the four stages of cost benefit analaysis? (4)

25. What is the meaning of 'shadow price'? (2)

26. Explain 3 problems with cost benefit analysis (6)

Chapter 13 – Policies to Achieve Efficient Resource Allocation

CIE Year 2. All other exam boards Year 1 (AS)

1. Give three reasons/circumstances in which the government applies a tax (3)

2. Give two advantages of an indirect tax (2)

3. Give two problems with an indirect tax (2)

4. Draw a diagram showing the incidence / burden of a tax when the PED for a good is inelastic (3)

5. Draw a diagram showing the incidence / burden of a tax when the PED for a good is elastic (3)

6. In order to reduce consumption significantly would PED need to be elastic or inelastic (1)

7. Explain why it is difficult for a tax to fully correct market failure (2)

8. Give two benefits of a subsidy (2)

9. Give two problems with a subsidy (2)

10. Explain why it is difficult to fully correct the market failure with a subsidy (2)

9. Define privatisation (1)

10. What are the two main reasons for privatisation? (2)

11. What is contracting out? (1)

12. Give an example of contracting out (1)

13. Give two problems with privatisation (2)

14. What is nationalisation? (1)

15. Give two reasons for nationalisation (2)

16. Define regulation (1)

17. Give two examples of COVID regulations (2)

18. Give two examples of regulation to increase consumption of merit goods (2)

19. Give two examples of regulation to decrease consumption of demerit goods (2)

20. Give two problems with regulation (2)

21. Define deregulation (1)

22. Give two reasons for deregulation (2)

23. Give two problems with deregulation (2)

24. In each situation which policy would be most appropriate - privatisation, regulation or deregulation? (5)

   a) a government run firm is inefficient

   b) increase the use of hand gel

   c) Increase competition in private industry

   d) Reduce the level of smoking in public areas

   e) Increase the use of green energy

25. Give three examples of state provision (3)

26. Why does the government provide each of the examples above? (3)

27. What are the two ways in which state provision could take place? (2)

28. Which market failure does state provision correct? (1)

29. Give three problems with state provision (3)

30. Give three problems with the state providing health care (3)

31. Give two examples of information to reduce a negative externality (2)

32. Give two examples of information provision to increase consumption of merit goods (2)

33. Give two problems of information provision (2)

Q34-38 not needed for AQA

34. Explain the concept of tradable pollution permits (2)

35. If a firm exceeds the level what are their two options? (2)

36. What are two incentives for firms to lower their emissions? (2)

37. Give two advantages of tradable permits (2)

38. Give two problems of tradable permits (2)

39. Define government failure (1)

40. Give two reasons for government failure (2)

41. For each situation state what the government failure could be (9)
a) Charging people to dispose waste

b) Age restrictions on smoking

c) Banning drugs

d) Maximum prices

e) Minimum prices

f) Subsidies to public transport

g) Congestion charges

h) Health and safety regulations

i) Stricter pollution controls

Chapter 14 Income and Wealth Distribution

CIE and AQA for micro.
This section is in the macro specification for other exam boards

1. What is a progressive tax? Give an example (2)

2. Explain one problem with a progressive tax (2)

3. What is a means tested benefit? (1)

4. Explain one problem with means tested benefits (2)

5. What is capital gains tax? (1)

6. What is inheritance tax? (1)

7. What is a transfer payment? Give an example (2)

8. Explain how the above taxes improve equality (2)

9. What is the difference between equity and equality? (2)

10. Draw a diagram of a Lorenz curve (2)

11. What is the formula for calculating the Gini coefficient? (2)

12. What does it mean if the Gini coefficient is 0? (1)

13. What does it mean if the Gini coefficient is 1? (1)

14. What is the poverty trap? (2)

15. Explain why means tested benefits increase the poverty trap (2)

16. Explain three positives of an unequal distribution of income (6)

17. Explain three problems with an unequal distribution of income (6)

18. Define absolute poverty (2)

19. Define relative poverty (2)

20. Give three causes of poverty (3)

21. Give three problems with poverty (3)

Chapter 15 Behavioral Economics

<u>AQA only</u>

1. What is the meaning of bounded rationality? (2)

2. Explain the meaning of bounded self control giving an example (3)

3. What is the meaning of cognitive bias? (2)

4. Explain the meaning of availability bias giving an example (3)

5. Explain the meaning of anchoring giving an example (3)

6. Explain the meaning of social norms giving an example (3)

7. Explain how a social norm can lead to people exercising more (2)

8. Explain the meaning of nudges (2)

9. Explain the meaning of altruism giving an example (2)

10. Explain the relationship between choice architecture and nudge using a canteen layout as an example (3)

11. Explain making use of an example the concept of framing (2)

12. Explain why restricted choice would be easier for consumers when it comes to choosing a mobile phone tariff (2)

13. For each question state whether it is an example of nudge or shove (5)
a) giving young people vouchers if they have the covid injection

b) Opting out of being an organ donor

c) Fining people who speed

d) Regulation to stop smoking indoors

e) Information provision on the benefit of exercise

	I understand this well	I struggled with some of this	This was really difficult so needs more work
Chapter 1			
Chapter 2			
Chapter 3			
Chapter 4			
Chapter 5			
Chapter 6			
Chapter 7			
Chapter 8			
Chapter 9			
Chapter 10			
Chapter 11			
Chapter 12			
Chapter 13			
Chapter 14			
Chapter 15			

Exam /Test Dates

Additional Notes

Additional Notes

Additional Notes

Additional Notes

Additional Notes

Additional Notes

Additional Notes

Additional Notes

Additional Notes

Additional Notes

Printed in Great Britain
by Amazon